The Phone Booth: a year in haiku and other writings

William G. Hobbs

ISBN 978-1-7380339-2-8

In memory of Joel

****

Dedicated to my film students
for all the haikus I made you write

and

to my wife, Sarah

who is this creature
industry wrapped in beauty
a life shared with mine

Table of Contents

Introduction

For Christmas in 2014, I received a small notepad. It was wire-bound and had a wooden cover with a print of a phone booth on it.

I wanted to do something special with this notepad. I didn't want to just use it for shopping lists and telephone messages and math problems. So I challenged myself to spend the following year and use it for writing at least one haiku a day.

Haiku is a japanese style of poetry. It is made up of seventeen syllables in three lines. The first and third lines have 5 syllables, while the second line has 7 syllables. Usually it contains no punctuation or capitalization. And traditionally 'nature' is the theme of a haiku, but I didn't limit myself as I wrote.

What unfolded were random thoughts and observations on current events, food, work, play, books, movies, life, death and whatever. It became a kind of journal. My wife, Sarah (SJH), even wrote a few. By the end of the year, I hated writing haikus and I set it aside. Occasionally, I pulled it out and used one in a note to someone.

In 2019, on a trip to Toronto, the back window of my SUV was smashed in and my backpack was stolen. The notepad was inside and I thought it was lost forever. Miraculously, I got it back. Not so miraculously, there were two notebooks of unfinished stories I'd been working on that I never got back. This led me to type out these haikus before they were lost again and in so doing I rediscovered them for myself. Now I want to share them.

Even though I mostly wrote one a day, I do not suggest you read it like a one-a-day calendar. Instead treat each month like a chapter and feel the flow of the seasons as you make your way with me through the year 2015.

For the Other Writings, I've included some old and new pieces that help flesh things out. First are two short stories I wrote in high school and had published in the school paper, *The Saints and Sinners,* in 1991 or 1992. They were the first of my 'phone booth' stories. I like phone booths. I have a small collection of souvenir ones. I guess it goes back to the Superman wallpaper I had as a kid; one of the images was Clark Kent changing in a phone booth. I remember being disappointed that I couldn't find many in our hometown – I think there was only one. As a glass box out in the open, it struck me that a phone booth is a place you could feel both claustrophobic and agoraphobic at the same time. The poem, *Somebody Call 911,* is a reworking of the first short story.

Next is my 'father-of-the-bride' speech for my girl who turned 16 during my year of haiku.

And finally, is the radio script of my play, *The Light of Christmas.* Why it is included will make sense when you read the month of December haikus.

Enjoy

William G. Hobbs
November 2024

p.s. Here is an extra haiku I wrote on the inside cover of the notepad.

Jan. 13

late night pay phone calls
your voice brings you no closer
where are pay phones now?

January

Jan. 1

a pad of paper
a christmas gift with promise
each day a new poem

Jan. 2 (from peterborough)

snow in the morning
fun games in the afternoon
long drive home at night
--
the good thing about
writing a haiku a day
is some can be bad

Jan. 3

five seven five is
the syllabic pattern of
haiku – now you know

Jan. 4

three lines like three acts
themes of cinematic scale
so small yet so grand

--

(Job 40:2)
questions and answers
Job wants answers – God questions
"shall you correct God?"

Jan. 5

i have not written
a poem today – what's the point
i'll try tomorrow

Jan. 6

cap'n jim has set sail
almost read it without tears
farewell house of dreams

Jan. 7

gun shots in paris
twelve dead for drawing cartoons
no laughing matter

Jan. 8

today just happened
i went to work – it snowed
not much to report

Jan. 9

today i am sick
should have stayed in bed all day
thursday is coming

Jan. 10

sore and achy neck
congested tired cough cough
give me rest tonight

Jan. 11

a short line of hope
a thought worth contemplating
a final landing

Jan. 12

puzzle on table
displaying a dream-like scene
Mia found that piece

Jan. 13

snowy winter day
little girls on an ice pond
nice pond an ice pond

Jan. 14

waiting room sitting
A-Ha on the radio
really hate that song

Jan. 15

beauty for ashes
out of the dust something good
a new beginning

Jan. 16

cheese pepperoni
delicious homemade love food
a slice of pizza

Jan. 17

crazy telephone
pancreatitis – lock-down
beyond my helping
--
good news with bad news
lego davinci's 'bot wins
dad needs to diet

Jan. 18

came to an inkling
old novels new to me
much reading ahead

Jan. 19

(Romans 11)
to show all mercy
God counts all of us wayward
don't be arrogant

Jan. 20

puzzle done but one
Mia found the missing piece
now joy is complete

Jan. 21

no news is good news
a sea of uncertainty
know more tomorrow?
--
dad is sick in bed
but message mixed calling home
they thought it was me

Jan. 22

what a day today
so many telephone calls
where's 'Young Sherlock Holmes'?

Jan. 23

hospital parking
ten dollars equals two hours
but I saw my dad

Jan. 24

bliss of feeling numb?
Satisfied or defeated?
The end of desire

Jan. 25

wonder why I call
trying to record a show
if i don't it's missed

Jan. 26

blueberry pancakes
perfectly fried with bacon
lunch all together

Jan. 27

(Philippians)
Rejoice in the Lord
and again I say rejoice!
Though I have sorrow

Jan. 28

snuggle and a kiss
goodnight my little mermaids
sleep sound in Jesus

Jan. 29

put things on a shelf
move things around in the house
reorganizing

Jan. 30

flowers for my mom
toilet seat shower soap rest
gave my dad a shave

Jan. 31

in the winter snow
it's very bright late at night
will I go to sleep?

February

Feb. 1

don't care for football
but the commercials are cool
super bowl sunday

Feb. 2

happy groundhog day
little mermaid turned seven
snow covered the ground

Feb. 3

download disc to drive
of digital memories
laptop treasure chest

Feb. 4

waves of nausea
fighting to hold up my head
but it could be worse

Feb. 5

target and redbox
both are leaving Canada
can't take the cold, eh?

Feb. 6

phantom radio
dashboard knobs and signal lights
intermittently

Feb. 7

the supreme court says
we're tired of your complaining
so die already

Feb. 8

occasionally
the syllables will count out
a line will appear

Feb. 9

chili – new people
perfect snowflakes on the glass
hot dogs freezing rain

Feb. 9

fluffy snow on ground
like dandelion seedlings
shovelling driveways

Feb. 10

God's foolishness is
wiser than human wisdom
the wise are no fools

Feb. 11

if remembering
changes memories – am i
still me and you you?

Feb. 12

some days are for rest
contemplation lazy fun
fight on tomorrow

Feb. 13

in order that you
understand how do i put
my thoughts in order?

Feb. 14

murder mystery
love and death on valentines
make a lucky guess

Feb. 15

what i did today
shovel snow and drive the kids
my go-to haiku

Feb. 16

reading by the fire
relaxing fun in the snow
winter at crossroads
--
the party's over
can't cry more if you want to
goodbye Lesley Gore
--
bacon cheeseburger
homemade juicy banquet feast
heaven on my tongue

Feb. 17

measles or weasels
i couldn't tell them apart
i had chicken pox

Feb. 18

looking like a fool
with poles and really long shoes
cross-country skiing

Feb. 19

little boy away
on the back of the north wind
a city in tears
--
i dream of high school
feeling now like i did then
i don't belong here

Feb. 20

heaviness sets in
bury my soul deep deep down
do what's to be done

Feb. 21

to the colourblind:
the sunset was beautiful
sorry you missed it

Feb. 22

what is worship
giving my first and my best
blessed be the Lord

Feb. 23

clinkety clink clunk
loonies from a change machine
twenty dollar tune

Feb. 24

early friday night
venus mars and crescent moon
tri-luminous awe
--
good ole buddy jim
hi – what – hi – what – hi – oh hi
good ole buddy jim

Feb. 25

(1 Cor. 6:12, 10:23)
all things are allowed
but not all things are helpful
be slavė to no thing

Feb. 26

i almost get it
but until i get it i
can't say what it is

Feb. 27

bare winter branches
silhouetted by sunset
doodle or design
--
live long and prosper
farewell to mister Nimoy
shalom spock shalom

Feb. 28

the big idea
of small ideas is to
birth big ideas

March

Mar. 1

hush of falling snow
scrape of shovel against ice
driveway sonata

Mar. 2

is it possible?
turning enemies to friends
growing good inside

Mar. 3

march came in not like
a lion or a lamb but
more like a wet dog

Mar. 4

march fourth marches forth
i'm not sure where exactly
march the fifth i guess

Mar. 5

full moon floods the sky
icy snow moon-mimicking
my birthday in morn

Mar. 6

why do i love thee
sweet savour melt on the tongue
medium rare steak

Mar. 7

fixed stuff and hung out
saturday was saturday
felt normal. it's weird

Mar. 8

words words words words words
we try to express ourselves
but words come up short

Mar. 9

sun shines and ice melts
we remember what it is
to be warm again

Mar. 10

love can be easy
or love can be a duty
my little children

Mar. 11

once upon a time
a boy dreamed that he could fly
very high. the end

Mar. 12

a wandering dream
hallways staircases and doors
searching for treasure

Mar. 13

this is unity
one body but many parts
together in Christ

Mar. 14 (03.14/15)

some say the Bible
has pi wrong. I say that is
just irrational

Mar. 15

turn the other cheek
break the cycle of violence
triumph by losing

Mar. 16

mondays start with groans
another week like the last
the wheels keep spinning

Mar. 17

i was second born
i've always liked tuesdays and
playing second base

Mar. 18

stuck in the middle
when will wednesday be over
when when someday when

Mar. 19

"This must be Thursday.
I never could get the hang
of Thursdays." "Drink up."
(adapted from *Arthur Dent and Ford Prefect "The Hitchhiker's Guide to the Galaxy" - Douglas Adams*)

Mar. 20

equinox starts spring
everything starts on friday
lights camera action

Mar. 21

stay in bed late or
watch cartoons all saturday
once upon a time

Mar. 22

the first shall be last
is sunday the beginning
or end of the week
--
watched mary poppins
and then we laughed and we laughed
but we didn't fly
(*Elisa, my daughter, said this as she was going to bed.*)

Mar. 23

strike spare gutterball
monday bowling symphony
wish we could play more

Mar. 24

lift the veil and see
be transformed from old glory
to the new glory

Mar. 25

choose words carefully
make friends and not enemies
everybody wins

Mar. 26

stuck in a big gym
with an air vent flapping like
a kite in the wind
--
to win learn or love
is life a struggle a school
or sacred romance

Mar. 27

magic books and dolls
clothes given a second chance
thrift store treasure hunt

Mar. 28

wishing and hoping
are not the same as doing
where's inspiration
--
freedom is just a
new kind of prison trading
master for master

Mar. 29

colt of a donkey
hosanna in the highest
Jesus is the king!

Mar. 30

hurricanes swirl
a colliding galaxy
of not stars but rain

Mar. 31

hail down some taxis
in an orderly manner
always keep your head

April

(For the month of April, I tried to write a series of haikus that all connect to form one story.)

Apr. 1

this is the story
of my friend Jacob Alley
born on april fools

Apr. 2

Jacob was not tall
or short, but only in height
was he average

Apr. 3

would I wish he was
like me or would I wish I
was like he could be?

Apr. 4

if I could be he
what would I see? would he see
he, if he were me?

Apr. 5

it snowed outside when
Jacob woke on Easter morn
hiding all the eggs

Apr. 6

Jacob barely slowed
as the gull bounced off the car
along the canal

Apr. 7

the gull flew away
Jacob continued to drive
to the desert's edge

Apr. 8

how long had he passed
through this desert wilderness
and what lay ahead?

Apr. 9

there may be giants
but for now a day of rest
and gathering stones

Apr. 10

rest Jacob Alley
the aDrAkoWy will come
you must be ready

Apr. 11

the aDrAkoWy
takes and takes giving little
it will squelch your dreams

Apr. 12

driving you crazy
making you tick the boxes
it has no feeling

Apr. 13

living for itself
cold life-draining like a shark
the aDrAkoWy

Apr. 14

Jacob took a day
catching trains catching fish and rays
and mending fences

Apr. 15

how to break the chains
to make a change for better
to find abundance

Apr. 16

to find the secret
to make master and slave friends
serving each other

Apr. 17

he dreams of flying
but in his life he cannot
find a way to soar

Apr. 18

he looks for a way
to be a superhero
the thought gives him hope

Apr. 19

a bike ride in rain
brings him crashing down to earth
cold wet and achy

Apr. 20

in life as on stage
a great word and a great death
are the best reward

Apr. 21

what's the point of life?
"meaningless" says Solomon
"like chasing the wind"

Apr. 22

a whiff of snow brings
rest from the aDrAkoWy
Jacob's mind awakes

Apr. 23

Jacob makes a plan
to tame the aDraAkoWy
make it be his pet

Apr. 24

consider it joy
Jacob, when you face troubles
then you can tame it

Apr. 25

find joy where you are
eclipse the aDrAkoWy
behind contentment

Apr. 26

the aDrAkoWy
stares back like a gaping void
it can wear him down

Apr. 27

swallow him away
take him from his most loved ones
leave him all alone

Apr. 28

most people give up
the aDrAkoWy's too strong
Jacob tries again

Apr. 29

rage rage rage Jacob
as if your raging matters
what's the difference?

Apr. 30

i will find a way
aDraAkoWy won't beat me
God help me, i will

May

May 1

if at first i may
seem distant, know i am here
on the first of may

May 2

campfire cooking
takes me back to the mountains
all the way out west

May 3

"I think, therefore I
am. I am, therefore God is."
said Rene Descartes
--
step into the light
no more secrets no more lies
be true be alive

May 4

bug-eaten bunnies
beneath backyard be buried
bye-bye brave bouncers

May 5

cobblestone of words
scribbles at the edge of night
make sense of the day

May 6

floating in cool sheets
under the dictatorship
of a soft pillow

May 7

why is there colour?
why beauty? why fantasy?
why such blissful dreams?

May 8

daydreams on a train
away from all the mundane
workday station stops

May 9

sweet mother of mine
any colour, but not pink
i've learned my lesson

May 10

milk or solid food
how can you be sure you are
digesting the meat?

May 11

can you help me, please?
brace yourself to brace the shelf
nicely to the wall

May 12

new comes out of old
it was always in the old
a hidden mystery

May 13

i can't remember
checking face in the mirror
and walking away

May 14

years and years go by
reconnect and carry on
happy birthday, Dave

May 15

this may day maybe
a rare time to be alive
five-one-five-one-five

May 16

magic of movies
pennies fly back to heaven
the lost can be found

May 17

no dreams are shattered
imaginations come true
some call it heaven

May 18

clickety clack clack
fingers dance on laptop keys
a story takes shape

May 19

wheels spinning in mud
no moving forward or back
need inspiration
--

who is this creature
industry wrapped in beauty
a life shared with mine

May 20

ring constricts finger
pulsing purple blood balloon
pliers cut it free

May 21

David Letterman
friendly giant of late night
close the castle gate

May 22

gathered together
a witness of promises
hand in hand for life

May 23

whirring lawnmower
cloud of dandelion fluff
made it out alive

May 24

hidden waterfalls
well explored trails of my youth
pete's dam memories

May 25

stretch across the sky
orange purple sunset clouds
like another world

May 26

late night under lights
out at first and take a walk
slap at mosquitoes

May 27

and now you are gone
right now i don't remember
when was the last time

May 28

numb and in a daze
Venus sets as I come home
gone to mystery

May 29

afraid of heaven
afraid there will be no more sleep
i love sleep so much

May 30

follow the arrows
take side streets and crescent turns
bargains on the lawn

May 31

lay me down to sleep
sixty times sixty times ten
floor food and phone calls

June

Jun. 1

rice is for display
rainbow trout on bed of rice
yoga mat more like

Jun. 2

does it look like him
his hair was different, but then
when was his hair not

(SJH)
joel was my nephew
his life done at twenty-three
letters never sent

Jun. 3

passing through shadow
let me carry your sadness
turn and i will heal

Jun. 4

being elected
there is no plan, but to keep
being elected

Jun. 5

dark clouds bring cool breeze
relief from the burning sun
blows the icy kiss
--
ladder next to roof
eavestrough full of maple keys
scoop scoop flutter down

Jun. 6

squeezed under the sink
contorted like houdini
i must hate phone calls

Jun. 7

curled up together
old romance in black and white
'til we meet again

Jun. 8

left on a jet plane
adventure of a lifetime
knee banged on table

Jun. 9

one day far away
not so empty here at home
empty nonetheless

Jun. 10

where are one and two
the bowling lanes start at three
gutter ball black hole

Jun. 11

sleep is for the weak
i wish i was not so strong
i could sleep a week

Jun. 12

tickets all sold out
don't want to miss the party
oh the irony

Jun. 13

high jump triple jump
run around the track, keep track
award out ribbons

Jun. 14

see you on the screen
talk to you like you are here
hold you but i can't

Jun. 15

one last night alone
one more day and you are near
home is home again

Jun. 16

is it really you
body mind another time
home but not back yet

Jun. 17

wait until tonight
so i did but now i must
wait 'til tomorrow

Jun. 18

lights cam'ra action
step into the make believe
pretend and find truth

Jun. 19

"if i had my way
i would tear this building down
if i had my way"
(adapted from *Samson and Deliah - Rev. Gary Davis*)
--
sat through prayer meeting
bullets pierce through all the blacks
can prayer pierce the whites

Jun. 20

dark rich chocolate
wheel barrow full of dirt
potato pillow

Jun. 21

it wasn't a dream
i saw me in a movie
on the big screen

Jun. 22

crash land for a day
hardball fast pitch to the shin
he's got a good arm

Jun. 23

make it go away
home is where i want to be
if i had my choice

Jun. 24

old Mister Alley
my imaginary friend
you listened so well

Jun. 25

on off back and forth
bicycle up down the street
papers to the door

Jun. 26

the worst of the worst
one is not like the other
abomination

Jun. 27

rain on my parade
clown makeup smudged on my cheek
water in my horn

Jun. 28

after years and years
contract three will no more be
oh what a relief

Jun. 29

little sunflower
lovely mermaid in my life
me your gummy bear

Jun. 30

exceptional needs
just to be ordinary
each little bit helps
--
round all the bases
green grass under bright night lights
essence of summer

July

Jul. 1

stargazer fireworks
jupiter passes venus
happy canada

Jul. 2

sunlight through the leaves
forest billows like a storm
myriad green shades

Jul. 3

ancient beautiful
alive calling whispering
spirit moves in words

Jul. 4

happy birthday Joel
you would have been twenty-four
no birthdays no more

Jul. 5

time to break away
running for the exit door
tie up loose ends

Jul. 6

run and kick the ball
use your head but not your hands
having fun's the goal

Jul. 7

yesterday i ran
today i can barely walk
too much fun can hurt

Jul. 8

all forgotten things
none worth turning back to get
forward vacation

Jul. 9

rough-cut misfit band
lob pitch hit homemat or car
hard-scrabble baseball

Jul. 10

set table say grace
pass the chicken pass the torch
dinner at gramma's

Jul. 11

strange shape up ahead
scrawny black bedhead bear cub
stares as we pass by

Jul. 12

solitary pole
rainbowed orb tethered to fly
spiral round and back

Jul. 13

lay down keep it straight
across and up nail in place
shingles keep off rain

Jul. 14

not because of me
i sit in Heaven with Christ
but because of He

Jul. 15

northern oasis
just off highway one-oh-one
wildwood bible camp

Jul. 16

mirror lake stillness
birdsong repeats on the wind
to rest in God's peace

Jul. 17

steam fogs up my eyes
cold water plunge shocks my core
sauna and cold lake

Jul. 18

drive drive drive drive drive
get up early barely stop
go go til you drop

Jul. 19

pizza factory
is the only place for me
in peterborough

Jul. 20

surprise at sunset
snapping turtle ancient green
lurches into lake

Jul. 21

lonely white birch tree
slants among the conifers
like a lightning bolt

Jul. 22

joseph's coat fabric
held by ropes stretched tree to tree
green leaves sway above

Jul. 23

bugs at breakfast time
mosquitoes in my pancakes
wouldn't change a thing

Jul. 24

achoo drip drip drip
sneezing like an elephant
on a summer's day

Jul. 25

middle of the night
street light looks like rising sun
sleeping in strange bed

Jul. 26

fumble for the key
do i really reside here?
end of vacation

Jul. 27

"i missed you" he said
in normal voice for others
but for him a shout

Jul. 28

routine and routine
in the grind chasing a buck
like watching paint dry

Jul. 29

arguing with her
as she with broken machine
was as effective

Jul. 30

sit down close the door
buckle up check the mirrors
first driving lesson

Jul. 31

sunshine to downpour
double rainbow and blue moon
there and back again

August

Aug. 1

stupid stupid day
pay to fix unbroken things
and things that don't work
--
old friends together
and now i don't feel so old
young again briefly

Aug. 2

just for a moment
we are children all again
smiles do not grow old

Aug. 3

space station surprise
speeding star across the sky
our campfire below

Aug. 4

flutter of colour
by me so close almost touch
like deep unformed dreams
--

butter of no cow
fly from flower to flower
whimsical creature

Aug. 5

The Princess Bride

giants miracles
revenge sword-fights and true love
inconceivable!

Aug. 6

go through the motions
my surreal reality
body there mind not

Aug. 7

how do weekends work?
tomorrow i will find out
hope i remember

Aug. 8

"and then what happened?"
the secret to a story
keep them wanting more

Aug. 9

is life a story
can we imagine great things
and make them better

Aug. 10

imagination
hope and dream so much could be
will it ever be
--
what has to be done
my mind and duty at war
trapped in attrition

Aug. 11

it seems to me that
to be taken for granted
is the highest love

Aug. 12

waiting takes so long
like a dream it is over
back waiting again

Aug. 13

connecting with God
each in our own unique way
as He made us all

Aug. 14

i couldn't help it
nothing personal – i laughed
automatically

Aug. 15

we are not the same
and so we need each other
it was meant to be

Aug. 16

power to shape minds
carried by storytellers
so often abused

Aug. 17

best – do something right
second best – do something wrong
worst – to do nothing

Aug. 18

key hook and bent nail
twisted into corner
open door come in

Aug. 19

To Kill a Mockingbird

scout searches for boo
evil is not black and white
do not judge by looks

Aug. 20

put it into words
a place a feeling a smell
words are not enough

Aug. 21

those nights long ago
a wee beastie in my bed
safe in daddy's arms

Aug. 22

grab a bowl and spoon
fruit toppings frozen yogurt
the joy of summer

Aug. 23

good work by a jerk
divide the man from his work
the work still stands strong

Aug. 24

when all goes crazy
try to keep your sanity
hide it if you must

Aug. 25

no one knows my name
extra work when i should play
forgot to tell me

Aug. 26

vester's got a gun
allison and andy down
live news is bad news

Aug. 27

deep wonderful sleep
wash away the stress of day
sleep deep dream deeper

Aug. 28

enjoy the summer
it is almost september
around move the stars

Aug. 29

rubber on pavement
little girl looks back and smiles
daddy come catch me

Aug. 30

Jesus is the key
and the lock and the mansion
it all turns on Him
--
you can't trust the book
only the man in the book
just don't trust the book

Aug. 31

take a second look
classic books old movie discs
treasure hunter's bliss

September

Sept. 1

time-travel doctor
screwdriver to fix not fight
who knows who you are

Sept. 2

big country buffet
soup salad chicken prime rib
keep going for more

Sept. 3

hazards in workplace?
work is a safety hazard!
best stay home in bed

Sept. 4

"Do You Believe?" (movie review)

twelve boring stories
intersecting each other
do not get better

Sept. 5

brand new computer
one terabit of memory
how long will it last

Sept. 6

happy birthday don
thirty-nine and still so young
fifteen since you've gone

Sept. 7

long night of sweet dreams
to sleep in on a monday
cuddle on the couch

Sept. 8

all sales are final
another store closes shop
Sears leaving sunday

Sept. 9

my girl can't decide
menus shoes clothes things of life
don't ask her advice
--

my girl can't decide
menus shoes clothes things of life
she don't get to vote

Sept. 10

fun day out at work
everyone loves marineland
five flipping dophins
--
sad lonely kiska
swimming around in circles
longing for the sea
--
playful belugas
underwater football game
chirping catching tires

Sept. 11

do you remember
eleven september
world trade towers fell
--
eye of a needle
mending holes sewing just so
last another day

September 11

When I learned that the nursery rhyme, Ring Around The Rosy, was about the tragedy of the Black Plague, I thought there should be a nursery rhyme to mark the tragedy of 9/11. So I wrote one.

One, Three, Five
Seven, Nine, Elelven
Here come the airplanes
To take us all to heaven

One, Three, Five
Seven, Nine, Elelven
Here come the airplanes
To take us all to heaven

One for those who are lost
Three for us who are left
Five for the sides of a pentagon
Seven for the day we can't forget

One, Three, Five
Seven, Nine, Elelven
Here come the airplanes
To take us all to heaven

Sept. 12

twirling noodle strings
spin to gold in keaggy's hands
just doin' nothin'

Sept. 13

poor meek and hungry
the kingdom the earth are yours
blessed you shall see God

Sept. 14

sad? take Latuda
but muscle twitch may result
the name makes me laugh

Sept. 15

shadows blind the world
sit and complain that it's dark
or turn on the light

Sept. 16

desperate to laugh
relieve this tension headache
to be meaningful

Sept. 17

school does not prepare
so they make work more like school
pointless paper work

Sept. 18

remember to stretch
one foot forward then switch feet
now do it faster

Sept. 19

rain mud and steep hills
a nice long walk by myself
trails of the gapper

Sept. 20

start soft slowly build
intense intense then flatline
make important point

Sept. 21

bags bags plastic bags
check for holes reuse for trash
recycle the rest

Sept. 22

you must play the pipe
it's as easy as lying
as you would play me
(adapted from *Hamlet – William Shakespeare*)

Sept. 23

standing at the lights
somebody else's problem
what world am i in

Sept. 24

air air losing air
fighting hard to stay awake
let me fall asleep

Sept. 25

a strength not his own
out of the strong something sweet
life riddled away
--
The Sting

finger beside nose
dress up take-down ruthless rich
the confidence man

Sept. 26

Potatoes

gold hidden in black
dig root them out wash them clean
boiled mashed and buttered

Sept. 27

my God oh my God
why have you forsaken me
is there an answer

Sept. 28

rich or destitute
all things are for enjoyment
everybody dreams

Sept. 29

The Taming of the Shrew

kate would be her own
but her rage leaves her alone
kiss! that's all he wants

Sept. 30

organization
pack repack and pack again
move around the dust

October

Oct. 1

the old cliché lines
like talk from a pull-string toy
words without meaning

Oct. 2

she said she'd be there
the door was locked the lights out
no fire plan today

Oct. 3

hot banana bread
melting butter spread on top
vanilla flavour

Oct. 4

blessed are those who mourn
there is hope comfort will come
from tears to dancing

Oct. 5

check off the list
the burden seems lighter now
what will they add next

Oct. 6

friends with a killer
is he reformed or waiting
is trust possible

Oct. 7

mental distraction
here there and the other place
or maybe not here

Oct. 8

locked in a prison
yet infinitely free with
imagination

Oct. 9

hats wigs teeth and scars
blood capes helmets and makeup
time to play dress-up

Oct. 10

these signs of autumn
gold nuggets out of the black
potato harvest

Oct. 11

magnify the Lord
thanksgiving is the microscope
see how good He is

Oct. 12

floating on the wind
fluttering rainbow wings
fly pull the string fly

Oct. 13

leaf corners pages
turn and turn and turn again
one day at a time

Oct. 14

blue jays and rangers
one long strange game five end six-three
let's go toronto

Oct. 15

ten fifteen fifteen
three dollar bus ride to work
eggrolls at the mall

Oct. 16

practice makes perfect
no good to know but not do
discipline's secret

Oct. 17

early morning dance
Venus Jupiter and Mars
Mercury in clouds

Oct. 18

crank turn chop chop grind
apples smashed smooshed pressed and squished
mining liquid gold

Oct. 19

hold nose and check box
animal alliance what?
parties win we lose

Oct. 20

red tide in morning
goodbye true dough meet trudeau
put it on credit

Oct. 21

back to the future
today is not like that day
where's my hoverboard

Oct. 22

stories all around
one starts as another ends
catch them if you can

Oct. 23

a cheap novelette
pick them up and put them down
goodness that's awkward

Oct. 24

one more then three free
just make it through tomorrow
three days to be me

Oct. 25

words lose their meaning
say it over and over
an empty echo

Oct. 26

tidy the clutter
organize to create space
dispel the chaos

Oct. 27

story needs all three
beginning middle and end
otherwise - "that's it?"

Oct. 28

lonely rainy day
patch fix basement antenna
clean out the eavestrough

Oct. 29

time and cars pass by
those moments where do they go
waiting for a bus

Oct. 30

(1 Corinthians 7)
to marry or not
don't worry you have not sinned
an unbeliever

Oct. 31

tardis doctor who
police public phone call box
old new borrowed blue

November

Nov. 1

to the rest i say
individual believers
stay as you are now

Nov. 2

if i could sing songs
if i could paint a picture
would i be happy

Nov. 3

make words mean something
natural speech – free on the streets
waste not one word more

Nov. 4

(movie titles)

stranger than fiction
big fish rope up paper man
it happened one night

Nov. 5

give us a surprise
but one that is expected
no cheating allowed

Nov. 6

sweet sixteen surprise
square dancing the night away
shocking tears of joy

Nov. 7

square dance hangover
slept-in but it's not enough
need an extra day

Nov. 8

lost in translation
meaning 'born again' he wrote
your son has expired

Nov. 9

today is sunny
a good day to rake leaves
tomorrow is rain

Nov. 10

style but no substance
a master of artistry
with nothing to say

Nov. 11

do you remember
forget the rest of the year
will it ever end

Nov. 12

voices in my head
they have stopped talking to me
no ideas now

Nov. 13

city of lights dark
hostage attacks explosions
chaos in the streets

Nov. 14

saturday to do
as little as possible
that's what's on my list

Nov. 15

have mercy in mind
mercy wins over judgment
justice is still served

Nov. 16

bowling and laundry
throwing strikes and cleaning up
gutter ball clothes pin

Nov. 17

adverbs are not friends
suddenly nothing happened
who needs suddenly

Nov. 18

too far and too much
florida out the window
please help me elvis

Nov. 19

nothing personal
feelings hurt but feelings heal
we each act our part

Nov. 20

power adapter
shoot video forever
no dead batteries

Nov. 21

communication
what i say and what you hear
not always the same

Nov. 22

things aren't so bad and
that's pretty good because we
know they could be worse

Nov. 23

what they say is true
art should only show the best
real life is boring

Nov. 24

bedroom invasion
antique-double-door wardrobe
wood-grain nebulae

Nov. 25

one month til christmas
bedroom wardrobe looms at me
where did the time go

Nov. 26

stumbling in a fog
can't make anything happen
always have to wait

Nov. 27

first read instructions
second open can – but wait
they are in the can

Nov. 28

what is in the frame
nothing else will matter but
what is in the frame

Nov. 29

(Isaiah 66)
sacrifice a lamb
as if breaking a dog's neck
meaningless worship

Nov. 30

Charlie Brown Christmas
fifty years on tv with
Linus and Lucy

December

During this month I directed a video of my play, The Light of Christmas, for my church. Many of the following haikus are about that. The script is included at the end of the 'Other Writings' section. You can see online how the play ended up by using this link: https://vimeo.com/149967928

Dec. 1

winter spreads darkness
christmas marks the light's return
Jesus is the light

Dec. 2

super hero dude
"the Eight Ball" - only power?
leave him last or lose

Dec. 3

there's no guarantee
give it your best and your all
for Him not for you

Dec. 4

cover up mistakes
zoom in switch focus snip snip
no one will notice

Dec. 5

stop move stop move stop
paint and clay tell the story
the light of Christmas

Dec. 6

in science fiction
write the inevitable
amaze your readers

Dec. 7

what's today's haiku
i can't think of anything
star wars is coming

Dec. 8

"and now here we are"
right line wrong time makes me laugh
makes everyone laugh
--
trays deliver plates
up down the aisle back and forth
dizzy dinner dance

Dec. 9

one half of one sock
whatcha gonna do with that
cover one half foot

Dec. 10

mae lynne my daughter
ding dong merrily on high
just now i see you

Dec. 11

somebody messed up
i'm not saying who it was
but it wasn't me

Dec. 12

animals from clay
two goats three kids one pony
stop-motion gives life

Dec. 13

christmas turkey drug
take a drumstick take a nap
pass out on the couch

Dec. 14

that wasn't so hard
it came quicker than i thought
not sure i did think

Dec. 15

ten days til christmas
so much shopping still to do
where did the time go

Dec. 16

candle in window
snowdrifts outside in the night
will the light shine through

Dec. 17

bloopers all day long
everyone forgets their lines
you just have to laugh

Dec. 18

the force awakens
not as strong as darth vader
kylo is afraid

Dec. 19

pandemonium
five days until christmas eve
and no place to park

Dec. 20

sail boat on the clouds
humpback merges with the land
nothing what it seems

Dec. 21

knit with sister-love
warm and cozy christmas socks
they fit perfectly

Dec. 22

head full of strange dreams
splitting migraine all night long
blue bike crew murders

Dec. 23

midnight gift-wrapping
christmas from the other side
joy of parenting

Dec. 24

no flakes on the ground
twas the night before Christmas
no snow to be found

Dec. 25

stockings on pillows
presents under Christmas tree
four points dry turkey

Dec. 26

early morning deal
parking if you are lucky
better to stay home

Dec. 27

gramma and grampa
playing games and laughing lots
family is such joy
(SJH)
--
boxing day take-out
lucky dragon chicken balls
chop suey for nine

Dec. 27

red blue yellow green
patterns of squares on attack
you block me blokus

Dec. 28

sing-along too long
stuck in some strange kind of hell
nuns versus nazis

Dec. 29

tuesday brunch with friends
snow and slush melting outside
playing games for fun

Dec. 30

tying up loose ends
searching for wooden handrail
and a can of paint

Dec. 31

what the future holds
a heart has to break sometime
never gets easy

(I don't remember why I wrote this last one. wgh 2024)

Other Writings

Fingerprints on the Glass

Heartbeat. The heartbeat. It pounds in my ear. Now it rings in my head. It reminds me that they're still alive and it proves their mortality. They won't listen to me, but it's my fault.

I don't remember when I entered. I don't remember why. And as the clock approaches twelve I realize how much time I've wasted. But will the clock reach twelve? It seems to take its time; too scared to go forward; too terrified to stop.

No one could waste time like me. No one could waste talent. 'If you don't use it, you lose it,' and I've lost my voice. I can no longer say what I think, for I always thought before I spoke and said nothing.

I wanted to save the world. That's why I came in here. But then I realized that I didn't really care whether the world lived or died, that there were just the few around me that I wanted to come along. I've let them go too, though. And now slime, pennies and slime are all that I get in return for listening to their heartbeat. I won't be able to listen soon.

He'd slid the pizza through the crack above the door and asked me how I was or if I needed help. I said that I was fine and to keep the change. Now I regret.

There's water on the floor. It's not mine; I know. It's raining outside. It's dark, but for the lightning. It's cold. The door still won't open and the windows won't break (oh, how I've tried!). I'm trapped.

“Stupid!” My own voice startles me, but I don't feel so alone anymore.

"This could only happen to me! Did Moses get stuck in a phone booth? No! Did Daniel get stuck in a phone booth? No!

"He did get stuck in a lions' den though." And Jonah got stuck in a whale, so a phone booth isn't so bad. It's isn't very magnificent either.

'WELCOME TO THE LAST CHAPTER,' reads the graffiti. 'STARTS FRIDAY.' I hate phones.

It's dark. The water is at my knees. The pizza's gone, my chocolate bar is half-eaten. The lamppost outside doesn't give much light. The rain and lightning are worse and Information keeps telling me that the sun is shining.

I want out... I think. It's safe in here. Peaceful. I suppose I could learn to sleep standing up. I could listen to my radio... 'til the batteries run dead. Safety is lonely. I have to get out.

"Oh, God, please get me out of here. So be it."

The phone is ringing.

"Hello," all I hear are sweet breaths. "Hello?"

"Oh, hello, there you are."

"Yes, here I am. What are we going to do about it?"

"It's good to hear your voice again. How've you been?"

"Cold and wet and alone and trapped. I've been eating though."

"Yes, well, you always do. Why do you keep hiding?"

"I... I don't know. I hate being out in the open where everybody can see me."

"I know the feeling. Well, stick with me; strength in numbers, you know; who can be against and all that. We should get you out of there, shouldn't we?"

"Please," the lamppost begins to brighten. "I'm sorry."

"Don't be sorry. Try harder. Keep close."

The door opens, but am I ready to leave my... coffin. It's time to go. Through the water to the land. It's time to...

Starts Friday

"Hey, you there, sir. Come up here."

"What?" I look up the street to see a large, well-built, well-dressed man.

"Come up here, sir. The movie's about to start. The stage curtain is open and the trailers are almost finished." Now I notice the theatre marquee above his head:

PATMOS THEATRE

- THE LAST CHAPTER -

STARTS FRIDAY

While the usher is on dry ground, the water is at my knees. I remember myself.

"We have to get out of here, there's a flood coming!"

"Not this time, sir. No. They're due for a dry, hot spell. Come, the movie's starting," he says as he leads me inside.

Except for the usher and me, the theatre is empty. The auditorium glowing bright from the film that has now started. I sit in the front row.

"Ya see, kid, it's pictures. It's all pictures." I would spill my drink, if I had one.

"Where did you come from!" A strange man is next to me in a

bright yellow tuxedo.

"Hey, you sat beside me. Good grief. Take a pill. You'd think you owned this place." He has popcorn.

"I'm sorry. What were you saying?"

"I was just saying that it's all pictures."

"What is?"

"Everything. A rock is a picture. A sparrow. A flower. A--"

"A picture of what?"

"Truth."

"What is truth?"

"Truth is!"

"Truth is truth?"

"True."

"Truth is true."

"One of the only two philosophical absolutes."

"Huh?

"It is an absolute that truth is true and it is an absolute that there cannot be no truth."

"Why not?"

"'Cause then you could truly, absolutely say that there is no truth. Which is a contradiction in terms."

"Huh?"

"Watch the movie."

The screen is a collage of death and violence, backdropped by sinking islands and crumbling mountains. A bloody moon and a charcoal sun chase each other back and forth across a starless sky in a race to beat time. I see people scattering in panic. I watch those terrified faces as they are devoured by hideous black monsters and demons. And now these dead bodies rise up, walk out of the screen, and sit around me in the auditorium. But others on the screen fade into shadows.

Now I look more closely at those faces. I recognize them. They are my friends, my family. The strange man beside me offers some popcorn. I accept.

It tastes good. It tastes excellent. It's the best popcorn I've ever tasted. I look back to the screen. My friends and my family. I suddenly feel sick.

“Here am I,” I whisper as I leave my seat and approach the pictures.

“Bring 'em back alive, kid.” Who was that strange man? My hands pass through the screen like fog.

“Hey!” a woman's voice. “Don't be such a loner!” As I turn to see her form approach me, I am struck by the light of the projector. I blink... and open my eyes to find the sun coming through the window.

Could it all have been a dream? The phone booth, the man in the yellow tuxedo? 'It's pictures,' he'd said. 'It's all pictures.'

I get up and walk to the mirror. As I look, for an instant I can see the light of the projector and the ones in the audience. I am a picture. I am no longer a spectator. I am art. I am a paint brush. The painting I am in and affecting has been kicked around and beaten and left in the mud and now, now it is time for it to be restored to its original innocence.

* * * * *

Somebody Call 911

The clouds were brown and dirty
Balls of floor dust in the sky
An impenetrable ceiling of doubt
And the rain fell as if the sun had never dawned

People going to and fro
Under the dirty, brown clouds
A city of need where stood a glass box,
Under the clouds, a candle lit deep inside

Mud and grease and obscene words
Turn the windows into walls
The candle radiates all that it can
And the people march by, fighting lost mindwars

Indeed, the war is over
And the people are prisoners
Slaves to darkness, dirt and mundane routine
The light to freedom in an unnoticed box

W.G.Hobbs, 1997

This was published in 1997 in Iron Filings, issue #7. Iron Filings was/is a poetry newsletter created by my friend, Daniel Jarvis.

A Marriage Fable

My eldest daughter, Rowena, got married in June of 2024. Sadly, the groom's father was not in attendance. He had passed away the summer before within weeks of the engagement announcement. It was with this in mind that I wrote my father-of-the-bride speech...

Rowena, the week you were born, I started reading *Treasure Island* to you. That didn't work out so well. You kept falling asleep. But over the next several years I read a lot of books to you. Dr. Sueuss, *The Lion, The Witch and the Wardrobe* and all the Narnia books; The *Little House on the Prarie* books; *The Hobbit*; *Anne of Green Gables; Charlotte's Web.*

So on your wedding day, I thought I would tell you a couple more stories as you and William begin your life together.

This first is more a fable; a fable about a marriage. An odd marriage of an odd couple. Odder even than Felix and Oscar.

You see, not many people know this, but Grief and Joy are husband and wife. And surprisingly, it is a good marriage. That is why *sometimes* we cry at weddings and laugh at funerals. And it's good to cry at weddings and laugh at funerals. Say that with me - "It's good to cry at weddings and laugh at funerals."

Now you can be forgiven, if you didn't know that Grief and Joy are husband and wife. It comes as a surprise to many people. They are very different. For instance, Joy loves all kinds of food. She loves the smells and the flavours and the aromas. Loves it. Grief – not so much – he has a lot of sensitivities and allergies. He has that gene that makes cilantro taste like soap. So he's really picky with what he eats.

Grief is more introverted. He doesn't like crowds. But to be fair, crowds don't much like him either. Joy is extroverted. She loves parties. And they both go. You'll usually find Joy on the dance floor, while Grief is in a corner reading a book or at the snack table seeing if there's anything without cilantro – or onions. He doesn't like onions. You'd think he would, because onions make people cry, but he doesn't like them. To him, those are false tears and he thinks people are making fun of him. He had a rough childhood. People didn't really want him around.

Times being what they are, the two have very different day jobs. Joy works at general happiness – you know, birthday parties, karaoke, and I understand she has a thriving personalized cupcake business. Grief has a job as low-level frustration – this includes politics, obviously. He works part-time as a dental hygenist – and he's not very good. He can never freeze the nerve with the first needle and it always takes two or three. He did have a very promising career in country music. He wrote a lot of good hurtin' songs. But that is not who they really are. That's just their day jobs.

No one is sure how they got together. But, like I say, it is a good marriage. Joy without Grief can be selfish and rude and she tends to burn herself out. Grief without Joy is lonely and miserable. But there is a special love that binds them. Together they have a quiet peace. They are like a little boy with a kite. Joy loves to fly, but without Grief to hold the tension on the string, she comes crashing to the ground. Watching her fly is the one thing to lift his eyes to the sky. Love is the wind that makes it all make sense.

Yet people are always trying to separate them. Even though they are married, Joy still gets proposals almost every other week. Seems there is always someone who wants to have Joy all for their own. But anyone who wants Joy and isn't willing to share her, gets Grief. And Joy is devoted to her husband. If you try to avoid Grief you will find that you lose Joy too.

I think that is the point of this little fable. If you want to have Joy in your life, then don't be afraid to get close to Grief. For when they are together, Joy is never more beautiful and Grief is never more noble. And it is at times like this, when loves brings them together that Joy will cry and Grief will get up and dance.

And that's why it is good ...

That story is from me. As this day approached, I couldn't help but think of the loved ones that should be here, but can't. I'll mention two.

William, I only really met your father once, when we all had a lovely three-hour 'meet the parents' lunch. I could tell, Clarence, looked forward to this day and rejoiced.

Rowena, you are the same age now that my brother, your Uncle Don, was when he traded in this earthly adventure for the heavenly one. You are about to start the one adventure, the adventure of marriage, that he wished he could have.

So my next story is one that I think he would give if he was here. It is not something he actually ever said, but I only know it because of him. I will tell it as I heard it, as I think he would have done, because he was great at imitating people. It goes like this.

...and then, in a horrible Scottish accent, I told the funniest story I know.

The Light of Christmas

By W.G. Hobbs

(Original radio broadcast script – first broadcast December 24, 2006.)

Original cast

Danielle....................Rachel Brooks
Kurt..................................Tim Plett
Mom............................Sarah Hobbs
Dad/shepherds........................WGH
Announcer....................Ron Hughes
Mary/Dorcas..........Deborah Piggott
Joseph/Joe.....................Noel Bondt
Angel Gabriel..............Laura Halek
Wiseman 1..........Robert McDougal
Wiseman 2......................Bob Halek
Innkeeper....................Frank Webb

Twas the night before Christmas… (SFX: Christmas music in the background)

Danielle: Maub, do we hab anymore tissues?

Kurt: (mimicking) Maub, do we hab anymore tissues.

Danielle: Stob it!

Kurt: Stob it!

Mom: Oh, are you not feeling well?

Danielle: I'b tick.

Kurt: I'b tick.

Mom: Oh, right before Christmas. Well, I think there's another box in the closet. And take some vitamin C. And put a sweater on.

Danielle: (sneezes)

Kurt: And get the mop!

Danielle: (huffs at Kurt.)

Kurt: (huffs back)

Danielle: Stob it!

Kurt: Stob it!

Danielle: Kurt!

Kurt: Kurt!

Danielle: Maub!

Kurt: Maub!

Mom: Kurt, leave Danielle alone.

(sfx: front down opens, sounds of a blizzard outside.)

Dad: Whew! It's a cold one out there tonight. Whoever wanted a white Christmas got their wish. (sets down packages and stomps the snow off his boots.)

Mom: Oh! You're covered in snow. Let me help you.

Dad: (taking off coat.) Yeah, it's really coming down. Ah-ah-ah! That's okay. I've got those. No peeking. Got all your presents just in time for Jesus' birthday.

Kurt: December 25th isn't Jesus' real birthday, you know.

Dad: Yes, I know. I know. Nobody really knows what day it was.

Kurt: It's just a pagan holiday celebrating the winter solstice.

Dad: And what's that?

Kurt: What?

Dad: The winter solstice?

Kurt: December 25th. Roughly.

Dad: Yes, but what is it?

Kurt: I don't know.

Dad: It's the day in the northern hemisphere with the least sunlight or the longest night. People would light bonfires and make lots of noise in the hopes of bringing back the sun. In a sense, the winter solstice is the celebration of the return of the light. So that makes it a perfect day to celebrate Jesus' birth as a baby on earth.

Kurt: Why?

Dad: Because Jesus is the light of the world.

Kurt: (pause) And Santa Claus gets his red and white suit from a certain soft drink company that I will not name because I have no intention of promoting them in anyway whatsoever.

Dad: So what's your point?

Kurt: It's all about commercialism and there is nothing special about the day at all!

Danielle: It's spedal if we mate it spedal.

Kurt: It's spedal if we mate it spedal.

Dad: Oh, Danielle, have you got a cold.

Danielle: I'b dying.

Dad: There you go, dear, (kisses her head) take all the sympathy you can get. (takes packages and heads down the hall.) Where's the wrapping paper?

Mom: Look in the closet.

Dad: (looks) No.

Mom: Oh. Maybe we don't have any.

Dad: (comes back into the room) What do you mean, 'we don't have any'?

Mom: I think I may have used the last roll.

Dad: What about the kids? Kurt, did you see anymore wrapping paper?

Kurt: I got Mom to wrap my stuff.

Dad: Danielle?

Danielle: I ordoored eberyting online and id cabe wrabbed.

Dad: (pause) Do we have any newspaper?

Mom: Check the recycling box.

(Dad heads doorstairs)

(SFX: power goes out. all background noise goes quiet.)

Dad: Hey!

Kurt: I didn't do anything.

Dad: Who turned out the lights? (SFX: step, bump, crash.) (Grunts.) (pause) OUCH!

Mom: (yells) No one, dear. The power went out. I'll get some candles.

(SFX: footsteps, shuffling through cupboards, lighting a match, lighting candles.)

Danielle: Arb you otay, Dab?

Dad: (comes upstairs) Yeah, I'm okay. Thanks.

Mom: There. I'll put one in the window, too, in case someone is lost wandering outside.

Danielle: Doob you tink ids terrorids?

Kurt: Yes, Danielle. Terrorist hijacked all the snowmaking machines from all the ski resorts. Then they focussed them all on our little town and made this blizzard to cause an electrical blackout.

Danielle: Id could habben.

Dad: No, honey, it's just a symptom of money-hungry electric companies that favour profit over the cost of maintaining their equipment.

Mom: And you wonder where Kurt gets it from.

Kurt: So what do we do now?

Dad: I've got an idea. (runs to the bookshelf) Aha! Here we go! Everybody get comfortable. (turns pages. Clears throat.) Marley was dead…

Everyone else: (sighs, moans) Aww Dad! No!

Dad: What?

Danielle: Shoubn't we check the radio to tee how long the power ids going to be ovv?

Kurt: Duh! The power is off. How can we listen to the radio?

Danielle: Duh! The radio we use for camping. Or we coub check on the car radio out-tide.

Mom: That's right. We should fill the bathtub with water. We have a gas stove, so we should be okay for cooking. (beat) Kurt, go look in the garage for the camp radio and whatever other camping stuff you think we might need.

Kurt: I'm on the job. (leaves)

Dad: I'll go check the car radio for the weather forecast and see how bad things are. (heads outside into the blizzard).

Mom: The food in the freezer will be okay for a couple of hours and luckily its winter, so if this lasts for a few days we can keep the food outside in the snow.

Danielle: A pew days!

Mom: It could happen.

Danielle: Aw! Dis inn't a Murry Chrimmas a' all.

(Music break as time passes)

Dad: (enters from outside – SFX: blizzard, door slam, stamp feet.) Brrrrr! It is not letting up.

Mom: What did the radio say?

Dad: Ah, honey.

Mom: What?

Dad: I left the lights on the car – the battery is dead.

Mom: Not again. What about the van?

Dad: I didn't check.

Kurt: (enters from the garage.) I got the camp stove and the lantern and I found the radio.

Mom: We shouldn't use the kerosene lantern in the house. We could get carbon monoxide poisoning.

Kurt: Oh yeah. Anyway, here's the radio. Did you know there are goats in the backyard?

Danielle: Goads?

Kurt: And a little horse, I think.

Mom: I'm not getting anything on this radio. I think the batteries are dead in it too.

Kurt: Did anybody give anybody anything with batteries?

Mom: No.

Dad: No.

Danielle: No.

Kurt: What do you mean, 'no'? Half the stuff on my Christmas list needed batteries.

Dad: Doesn't that radio have a crank generator?

Mom: Oh yeah. Let me try winding it up. (winds the crank. And tries the dial.)

Announcer: …power outages are reported all over the county. Even this station is currently running on our emergency backup generators. But hydro crews are on the job and say power could be back up later tonight. But the National weather desk forecasts continued snow until after Boxing Day – as much as 50 centimetres of the white stuff – and if more power lines come down many residents could be spending this Christmas in the dark. Police are urging people stay off the roads unless it is absolutely necessary. The snowploughs are out in full force, but drivers say they can't keep up with volume of precipitation. A reminder to those pulling out their gas generators, to not, I repeat, NOT use them indoors. They can cause a build up of carbon monoxide gas and be deadly. Keep listening to … (turn off the radio. Long silence.)

Danielle: Arb we going to freebe to deat?

Mom: No, of course not. Like I said, we've got a gas stove. So we can cook. I filled the tub with water. We've got plenty of food. I think I even found some stuff left over from Y2K.

Kurt: And if we get really hungry, there are goats in the backyard.

Danielle: Oh, dis is the worst Chridmas ever. I'b sick. Dere's no power. Dere's no heat.

Kurt: There's goats.

Mom: Danielle. It's okay. As long as we're together, we can still have a good Christmas.

Danielle: Bud whad nexd? Are we going to get robbed?

(SFX: knock at the door.)

Danielle: Tee. Here dey come.

Dad: Robbers don't knock.

Mom: Someone must have seen the candle. (SFX: open door, blizzard, two people enter)

Dad: Come in. Come in both of you.

Joseph: Thank you.

Mary: We saw the light in the window.

Kurt: Why are you dressed like Mary and Joseph?

Mary: Because we are.

Mom: What?

Joseph: We're playing them in the living Nativity at the park. Or we were.

Mary: This evening hasn't gone like we planned. (gives out a moan of pain.)

Dad: Oh! Are you all right? Come sit down. Are you pregnant?

Danielle: Dab! Why woub you tink dat?

Dad: Typecasting.

Mary: No, I'm not pregnant. This is just a costume. (sits) Like Joe said, we were in the living Nativity at the park.

Kurt: Joe? Your real name is Joseph?

Joseph: Typecasting.

Kurt: Oh, so you must really be Mary?

Mary: No, my name is, Dorcas.

Kurt: (pause) Can we just call you Mary?

Mom: Kurt!

Kurt: What? It'll make it easier when we explain this.

Dad: (to Mary) Are you hurt?

Joseph: I think she may have broken her ankle.

Mary: It's just sprained.

Danielle: Wha 'abbened?

(SFX: - knock at the door.)

Mom: Who could that be? (SFX: – open door – blizzard – people come in and shake off snow.)

Dad: Let me guess – the Angel Gabriel, and you two look like wise men.

Gab: Yes.

Wise men: That's right.

Gab: Dorcas, are you all right?

Mary: I'll be fine, the snow broke my fall. How did you find us?

Gab: We followed your tracks.

Kurt: Did you lose one of the wise men in the snow? Shouldn't there be three of you?

Wise man 1: We're from a small church.

Wise man 2: And technically, the wise men didn't show up until around two years after the birth – according to Matthew – If we just stick to the very night of the birth, there's just Mary and Joseph, angels, shepherds and the innkeeper.

(SFX: – knock at the door)

Danielle: Now what? (SFX: – open door – blizzard – people come in and shake off snow.)

Dad: Well, speaking of shepherds…

Sheperd 1: We followed the tracks.

Kurt: It's getting kind of tight in here.

Mom: Well, the more the merrier. Everybody have a seat and I'll make some hot chocolate.

Wise man 1: Do you have any root beer?

Mom: Ah, no. Sorry.

Wise man 1: That's okay. I was just checking. Nobody ever has any root beer.

Shepherd 2: Dorcas are you all right?

Mary: Yes …

Danielle: Hold on a mibit. Wha 'appened? (sneezes)

Everyone: Bless you!

Danielle: Tank Cue. Now, can somebody tell me wha a libbing Natibity is?

Joe: Well, Nativity is another word for… (pause) What *does* Nativity mean?

Wise man 2: I think it comes from the Latin for birth, but don't quote me on that.

Kurt: I thought you were a wise man.

Wise man 1: He's not a real wise man, but he plays one at Christmastime.

Wise man 2: (flatly) Ha, ha.

Joe: Anyway, a living Nativity is when you act out the Christmas story from the Gospels. So, Dorcas and I were playing Mary and Joseph and we were on our way to Bethlehem.

Gab: I play the Angel Gabriel and I come to Mary and tell her that the Holy Spirit is going to conceive a child in her and that He will be the Son of God and that she will call him Jesus, because he will save his people from their sins.

Dad: You've been waiting all night to say that haven't you?

Gab: It was a lot of work memorizing my lines. I'd hate it to go to waste.

Joe: And then he comes to me in a dream and tells me the same thing so that I don't divorce Mary. And then there's this decree from Caesar that everyone has to go to the town of their birth to be taxed. So we get on a donkey and ride to Bethlehem.

Wise man 2: Except no one we knew had a donkey, so we got a pony and gave it fake ears.

Kurt: So that's your little horse in the backyard.

Joe: Yes.

Kurt: Are the goats yours too?

Shepherd 1: Those are mine.

Kurt: Aren't you supposed to have sheep?

Shepherd 1: In sticking to the story, yes. But I don't raise sheep, I raise goats.

Mom: The hot chocolate should be ready soon. So what church are you from?

Shepherd 1: The Church-of-making-do-with-what-you-have.

All: (laugh) Amen.

Danielle: So why arb you all here?

Joe: Well…

Gab: It's all my fault.

Mary: Oh, don't blame yourself. It was just a freak accident.

Wise man 1: It's probably more our fault. 'Cause, you see, we had set up the park like the little town of Bethlehem with the stable and the inn and the little houses.

Wise man 2: And we had Gab set up on this rigging and covered in Christmas lights so that we could have him fly around and make him glow light like a… like an angel. And since the wise men don't come on until later, Bob and I were manning the rigging.

Mary: And it all worked great.

Gab: Until it started to snow.

Wise man 1: See, we just had him hanging in the air and we would turn his lights on and off when it was time for his part. But the snow made the rigging really slippery.

Wise man 2: And he starts on one side of the park to talk to Mary and then while Mary and Joseph are on their way to Bethlehem we're supposed to move him over to the other side to talk to the shepherds.

Wise man 1: But we lost our grip and he flew right into the goat pen and the goats got loose.

Wise man 2: And then when we tried to correct we pulled too hard and he swung back and hit Mary on the pony.

Joe: And the pony took off running, dragging Mary behind in the snow and I tried to keep up and then Mary – Dorcas – fell off, but the pony kept going and the goats all ran after the pony. And we ran after the animals to get them back.

Shepherd 1: And then the lights went.

Shepherd 2: And now, here we are.

(SFX: – suddenly the power comes back on and everyone cheers!)

Everyone: Yay!

Danielle: Yess. We won hab to spen Chrimmas in da dark. (sneezes)

Everyone: Bless you.

Danielle: Tank cue.

Kurt: Wow. Dad, it's just like you said.

Dad: What?

Kurt: That December 25th is the perfect time to remember Jesus birth, because it comes at the time of year when we remember the return of the light. And now the lights are back on.

Dad: And Jesus is the light of the world.

(SFX: – knock at the door)

Kurt: I'll get it. (SFX:– open door – blizzard)

The Players: Hey it's Carl! (Carl comes in and shakes off snow.)

Carl: Hi, guys. It looks like they're finally starting to plough the streets.

Kurt: What part are you playing?

Carl: I'm the innkeeper.

Kurt: Really! Well, I hate to say it, but I don't think we have anymore room.

Everyone: (laughter.)

(Music up)

The End.

The Light of Christmas first aired as part
of the Family Bible Hour radio program.
Listen to it online at this link:
https://soundcloud.com/william-g-hobbs/the-light-of-christmas

www.ingramcontent.com/pod-product-compliance
Lightning Source LLC
LaVergne TN
LVHW041107150826
845673LV00007B/1960